HORIZONS
Collected Poems

**Poems
by
Jo Rippier**

First published in 2018 by Colin Smythe Limited
Gerrards Cross, Buckinghamshire SL9 8BA
www.colinsmythe.co.uk

British Library Cataloguing-in-Publication Data
A catalogue record for this book
is available from the British Library

ISBN: 978-0-86140-504-6

Produced in Great Britain
Printed and bound by CPI Antony Rowe Ltd, Chippenham, Wiltshire

Contents

7

Rooks

It is first of all the
noise, raucous at first
light, a loud insistent sound
which not only not annoys

in bed but conveys
a sense of life alive
dense filled fulfilled.
A day about to start.

How different later when the
birds black on dead trees
or like lees scattered singly
round the field lack

seeming purpose, stand
still, or search for food
till purposeless they have
consumed their fill.

Is this so unlike
much other life all
noise and rush, so aimless
in its flush, or strife?

And then once more at
night, the sound of rooks
still raucous, fading as they
united at last light.

The Stillness of Stillness

How still is still?
The slowness of a stone
tranquillity in still-life?

What remains quite still?
Eye of stabbing heron
the waters of a lake?

What quality is still?
The darkness of the night
mother's hand on child?

Where is stillness found?
Solace set in silence
the plucking of a lute?

And what is still left still?
The heart at rest
sounds of past remembrance?

Seasonal

It's hard not
to feel the fall
of falling leaves.

It's hard not
to suspect a sense
in leaves falling.

It's hard not
to feel leaves
falling fall

or avoid that
sense leaves
fallen leave.

Steam

Slow white presence
in a blue winter sky
ungainly its essence
fades to further stray.

Unlike hot air
these drops distilled
like true words spare
with meaning filled.

A plume on hold
controlled by man
not gods, unrolled
dispersed, and in its span

like true words
round in itself
the world rewards.

Mortal Coil

An outline meticulous distinct
as if ironed on to tarmac
skin colour almost still intact
and shining dully in the sun.

Unnatural still attractive shape
with tiny fingers on the point
hind legs at full stretch flattened
making one last full final thrust

A reminder of another frog
caught in the boat thrown
overboard from where it
fast swam towards the shore.

Unmoving but still visible
it rested on a rock
as if observing both
the point of its and our release.

Back to the first hours later.
There was now no shape just
wrinkling bulging sac, to
stop any further likeness lasting.

The Eye of the Beholder

Anything you look at
is what you have
in mind.

A woman
can mean murder
a flower growing rage.

The hunter and the
tiger may only see
their prey.

The artist looks inside
or round about
is open to what's there.

The critic looks
for what he knows,
can grasp, express.

A definition is
for one enough,
the other sees beyond.

Medieval Crucifixion

What others suffer
we behold:
pain on canvas
stretched down time.

And death, state sponsored.

The eye pitiless
records still
each racking twist.

Today we look
and merely see
a pain referred.

Each detail sharp
shows clear
though subject and
the Cross cross-fade.

Our sense is
cruel.
We feel what
they did not.

The wheel on
which they broke
was faith.

This fails us most.

Millennium

Suddenly
the past,
the comfortable past
is there no more.

What
lay behind
was always there,
could still be felt.

And now it's gone.

No
longer is
nineteenth, even twentieth
a century which means.

The
reality that
was, is now
virtual at click of mouse.

So
what exists
around us all,
just passes into space.

A
world not
brave, but on fast
fade, a screen flickering.

Today

There is no time like now
for now is now,
and now is what now is.

As for time, time
is as time was,
for now or ever.

And if time is
but never was,
what's now in fact is never.

Precious Metal

In itself
gold is pure

an essence clear
dross free.

Even heated
gold is soft

its glow warm
tempered steady.

Melted gold
forms golden tears

takes on other
gentle shapes.

Gold is never
angry ever

strikes no-one
hard or fast.

In itself
gold is pure.

Frozen Frame

You looked, I looked, and
you then passed me by.
A bridge too late, I stand
glance back and catch your eye.

Uncertain both we move, come close
shy distant years still part
till past warmth kindles, grows
and arms go out, a heart against a heart.

We walk together down the sands
sit firm on rock, hands
touching just, a reminiscent
faint and tingling shock.

Now sands of time in constant shift
soft blow across a timeless rift.

From the Distant Past

No tears

for tears are sad.
But why no tears?

Because there's hope?

No.
More a sense
that what was
is
and
what is cannot die.

So
though we live and love
apart

we cannot die.

The Amulet

If you wear this
think not of me

but
just

that this heart
holds you
to leave you free.

For Renate

Friendship is less than love
and more
for love is often here today
tomorrow gone.

Yet this friendship is
both near and far
as distance is no bar
to nearness of the heart.

It is no friendship
which exhausts expects
gives not, protects
itself by selfish wants.

Not like this friendship
which is just a simple fact
implicit held in understated tact,
a friendship unpretending, which just is.

On leaving

Never having known how
to arrive, for me each
end has been a start, a reach
for something sensed, now

close, now far, yet
beckoning, a waving hand or hazard,
the route uncharted, hard
perhaps yet not a threat.

And now this end, well, almost
end, before the end.
The final challenge, a test
of terms and time, to bend

the will, that unwilling will,
to face the worst, the last
the fading light, past
that post, last, beckoning still.

Autumn Sunshine

The beeches are no longer brown
but burnished
brandished torches
burning gold:

the darker limbs
aglow
with wetness shining:

all around
is lit
and lightened:

before that moment
when the sun will go.

A November Rose

It seemed a shame
to leave it
to the coming cold;

one last dark-red wrinkled bud.

I cut it long
and in the vase
it weakly glowed;

until the third day

when, opening a tiny crack,
it sent out
a fragrant sense;
faint reminder
of a summer day.

Late Robin

An untoward sound
in cold morning air
soft notes piercing
as from an other where:

off and across hard winter walls,
an echo: and plaintive
waking sense
of soft and other seasons past.

Time & Tide

Each day is long
as long as each day is.
It starts, begins
never, rarely makes its way,
no rhythm as the creak of age.

There is no urge or need,
just one more day
among the many
present, past,

the past still present
the future there,
as urges fade
and needs no more.

Acting

To be or not to be
is not the question.

Why should being
be a question, and
being someone else a deal?

If acting is being
someone else,
why be anybody?

Mansfield Park

can make one wonder
why one reads.

A novel mostly
sets one free
to wander in the mind
to make up the mind
from fantasy
and fiction.

Yet here
imperatives are implied,
a pressure subtle
but applied.

A will, the writer's
is here hard at work,
to pre-ordain, select, define.

Characters one likes
change seemingly, and are damned.
Duller, convention cling and huggers
are held up for praise.

Rank-breakers suddenly seem fun,
convention frigid, stiff.

And even if the good
do rightly win the good,
and goods, this still leaves
a sneaking, nagging
sense of somehow
having been let down.

For those few lasting moments

There is that certainty
that love is only sometimes,
never sometimes.

A word,
or look,
a softening of the eye

tells all,
is for all time,
cannot ever be denied.

Circumstances make the facts,
circumstances prison all.
one must rise above the facts

see clear,
be strong enough
to unshackle
common coils,

yet bear the load
that being free,
and being true,
involve.

Stolen Words

Now have you loved me one whole day,
tomorrow when I go what will you say?
For we have lived in that brief span
a life, lives,
and live.
Our vows, no vows, postdate
some newfound state.
For having purposed change
we now must part,
not falsehood.
Lovers' contracts bind but till sleep.
Vain lunatic, for one whole day you loved
for me now to go away.

Constellations

Yours is the love
that daily rises
with the sun.

The moon is mine
which each month only
lives to die.

I am the moon
in worlds of night
pale fellow of the day.

Your love is warm
as warm as love
that sunlike blows not cold.

The moon is bare.
With what sad steps
the moon tonight.

Time Past

Last night
all night
I spent with you
alone

I held you
kissed you
all alone

I found you
put my arms all round you
alone

And all alone
I leave you
but
not last night

Carte Blanche

The body is a map
of worlds
we see
and think we know.

Eyes wander
from sharp north
declining south
across round contours clear.

A surface
we so lightly over
look
shows not what lies beneath.

Or
who has been there
and if
when explored.

Like a map the body is
just there
a rendezvous for
all and
one.

Waiting Game

When we met first
were we not free and bound?
Now, later far, the worst
is to have found
that what then held us back
still puts us to the rack
of impulse, warm-willed,
but yet not even near fulfilled.

Distanced thus by time and ties
we smile and kiss,
look forward to . . . more lies?
Instead of what we still choose to miss.

Always

there will be regret
for what has been,
which now must let
in light to warm and wean

a newer time, yet still
be near to what has been:
a link to close and fill
that still close fading screen

on which our lives did play
so near to what has been:
a moment, moments, brief eternity,
before a now so clean.

We do not part, to part
from what has been:
you cannot part from heart to heart,
or what the heart has seen.

Always
there will be regret
for what there was has been.

The Power of Speech

Words
are always with us,
so often pass our lips.
They function, smooth our ways,
express, if not discuss.

For
words are there for all
of us. We catch a phrase,
an essence cutting through the maze
of meanings each word can recall.

You
and I use words
evasive, straight, direct
to say, unsay, perhaps distract
not touch discordant chords.

And there the matter rests:
uneasy state of truce
of words in search of truth
or further testing tests.

Kaiserstuhl in Autumn

A terrible beauty passes.
Leaves rattle
arid in the multi-coloured
sere
of decay.
A soft wind
chilling
tugs from what remains still quick,
late autumn's parting shreds.
Dust-puffs eddy round the fruitless trees.
Along the path
the grating nudge of maize.

No song-birds sing.
The bone-dry whisper in the trees
is hoarse;
a jay once sounds,
discordant on the wing.
Fettered vines
bound to stakes
motionless hang grave;
the fruit,
black clustered mutes.

All this combines
in nature's final show,
a season empty
with the blaze of total harmony.

Winter Day

How still the woods.
Morning
etched in cold
light on the grass.

No move, surround of fir
young, stiff
tips upward sharp.

Still feet sink,
mud
the only sound.

Wedge of empty downhill
swathe;
brand of man
clean cut to clear the slope.

Air invades,
corroding sense

and still the woods
move not.

February Test

Down dun woods water, unseen, sinks:
its soundless fall
a seeping course
white snowdrop lit,
through slow green covert moss.

Past tap-roots, into chalky down.
The fulcrum shifts.
Now weightless, water moves,
its heart, sky-open, bursts;
a welling constant steady beat.

Not dead, dispersed, the waters spill
rill-fast to early stream.
Cress-bedded, caught
by man's restraining hand
unchecked, but spinning currents flow.

Treacherous screens of leafless trees bare
gardens down to water's edge.
Perspectives, lawns, unhurried lines;
transparent nature bent
in formal studied natural grace.

Big houses, half-hid, merge. The rich
man's dream of country life
– the poor man's too –
unequal common sense
of something lost that never was.

The Nature of Love

I do not know the gardener,
the garden I have seen.
Not even hers, and like a modest lover
she hides behind a screen

of beauty, her own work all
yet natural, so doubly sweet.
A garden, secret, where honeysuckle
lingers, a golden rambling treat.

Flowers not seen by strangers' eye
they bloom for love; beyond that love
which only craves with raucous human cry;
love quiet, still, reversed to move.

Each year flowers in their season never
fail to make love passing last for ever.

Irish September

Somehow it seemed all wrong.
A road quivering with red
petals. Fuchsia falling
all along the way ahead.

Tarmac black beneath a sheen,
scarlet, crimson, claret?
Colours shifting in the sun;
cold, hot, a hardly merit.

To see is to believe.
But red fuchsia on that floor
is more than to conceive
nature is not rich but poor.

Gazing

When I looked up
I could see
high
in the sky silver.

Down and dark
I
one tiny spot
watching
as the bright band
along light
moved.

Behind
white trails of white
fading
into blue
above and in that sky.

Looking up the Loch

Rain points patterns
skims windblown
shadows
over
waiting water.

Granite
mountain greens
down
to water waiting.

Beyond,
beyond anything,
grey mist
enveils, mysterious,

beckoning
perhaps towards
more water,
waiting.

Echoes

Reeds in water, water weeds
water moving, swaying creeds
stems dipping half-bent bowed,
rippling screens, transparent cowed.

Reeds in water, water weeds
in water moving, ridden steeds
wind mastered, standing still
in silhouetted shadow drill.

Reeds in water, water weeds
light letting, where one reads
patterns shifting in the light
all clear, and yet barely bright.

Rubbing Along

Two pebbles in the mass
lie side by side
rest smooth, soft glide
on sand. Waves pass

to just lift these
pebbles from the rest
all roughness past.
Just two soft stones

all passion spent.
Two pebbles hardly soft
now rest often
yet together leant.

Red Admirals

On the bright road
they looked for all
the world like tiny sails
quick vibrant dark.

They passed beneath.
On looking back I saw
them scudding, like
sails flat on ice.

And then I knew.
They were not sails
they were not quick
their dark was now my dark.

Foxglove

The name alone awakes a sense
of woods soft heath night shade
of childhood dreams long past intense
when all else long since greyed.

With upward thrust the growth of age
a striving from the forest floor
slim rising plant green purple sage
warm quiet blooms a store

for 'humble pollinating bees'.
Such untimely passion thoughts
called up by just one word
from just one flower inferred.

The High Window

frames, catches birds that
pass. Some show against
the sky like missiles at
the strike. They miss each

time. Just swerve, are
gone. The crows slow
black on the wing flap
clumsy past the pane.

Last light marks
the parting of the day.
Birds fly no more in
that huge fading space.

Through glass darkly
I saw them,
wild geese
alone together.

Against dark light
darkening
they flew
in one.

The dark leader
thrusting
back to other
yearning wings.

I could not stay
to watch
as fast they
faded into dark.

Nor through glass darkly
could I hear
the sound of wild geese
calling calling . . .

Swifts

Sometimes they whisper
sometimes they scream
from daybreak to vesper
they streak dream
              or seem.

On wings curved like scythes
they cut and they cleave
or they dive while they weave
through air for their lives.

From here down below
earthed, firmly held down
rare watchers lone
a while take in this show.

Yet they will go home
on feet firmly based
to remember birds roam
in azure encased.

Brief Encounter

I walked along a busy street
inward turned and passing pale,
my thoughts all city, taut and neat,
and then I heard a nightingale.

Amazed I stopped, stood still
to ask, a vision or a waking dream?
It was no fancy passing, still
less what it might seem.

The voice I heard the rushing
passing crowd ignored. And
over traffic, hammer thud, its song
pure, piercing, like a strand

of hope, a hidden secret sound.
Yet passing clear in all that din
the tiny unseen bird was bound
and treed and held within.

A bird of passage, passing strange,
its message fading out of range.
I went my way, time to repair,
that song still ringing in the city air.

Lochside

Unquiet sounds from the edge
water lapping
shifting, tapping
tapping, as
at some door
invisible
insistent
unquiet sounds at the edge.

Levitation

What is it
about the wind?

That feel
and sense of endless
endlessness?

Always there,
or not.

A pulse,
a thrusting force
or waft, caress
across the face
unseen but gently felt.

The visible
theatrical effects:

September swallows
whirling like blown leaves

or, on wind-lashed trees, leaves
rippling like dervished silk.

What is it
about the wind?

Questions

Standing at a gate
pressed against the bar
a sense of being late,
light fading here, and far.

The hardness of the wood
through fabric to the heart
resists anything softness might,
should, or even could impart.

But does verse so restricting
permit just meaning clear?

Or just lines constricting
within a dwindling sphere?

Perspectives

Why is a still life
so rarely still?

The words alone
a contradictive clash.

And, let's face it,
action, battle scenes on canvas
often are just
colours, figures
frozen on a frame.

In contrast now a picture
of hibiscus in a vase.
One small shift of light or sun,
the flowers gleam and glow,
then as at sunset fade
like shadows, yet retain
that essence, stay quite
still but full of life.

Or in another vase
chrysanthemums, wilting,
gently evincing
that mortality which
accompanies all life
but which an artist
can make last, live on
for ever.

Simplicity

is when you think,
actually admit something
to yourself.
No shabby layers
of lazy compromising
doubt.

Just straight direct
unflinching thought,
without any of that self-restraint
imposed by
custom, habit, moral code.

That simplicity
electrifies, releases
elemental force
to act
in self
all doubts dispelled.

Such simplicity
enviable
desirable
so seldom found.

Lifeline

Nothing is for ever.
That's why we think it is.
We know, but do not
wish to face, or even look towards
a future everlasting mortal.

Instead we sing
the song of songs,
of love, life, and living,
for ever,
and ever.

Until the dimming dims.

Blake's Way

O worm, thou art lost
upon hard pave stone tossed.
But, from the grave,
this life will I save.

Not true, you were not tossed
but after rain had lost
your way. So why did I
not let you die?

Or permit you carry on your diresome way
till end had nighed, or by some bird
consumed, which is to say,
and nature's way inferred.

Thus we arrogating mortals
in our self-reflecting awe
like gods do ape immortals,
challenge nature's unrelenting law.

Catch and Release

How nice
if as with fish
arrangements
would just loosen
like a hook.

It is thought
that fish don't feel,
but humans do not
take to hooks.

They just hang on,
await release:

a practice which,
in both fish
and man,
is false.

Uncertainties

'A poem should rhyme,
scan, and make sense.'

It should also be of its time,
mean, even make one tense.
But poetry should also reflect
life, which rarely scans,
often can be more than tense,
and as for making any kind of sense
that is what a poem does,
or should. Or could.

How can this paradox
be resolved?
For words, like life,
do not stay the same
and rarely make a twinlike fit.

All the poor scribe
can hope to do
is, lonely, unscanned,
always tense,
go for what some inner sense
impels
on to the printed page.

Playing with Water

Love is never single
and the waters have cooled.
Hurt and hate can overrule,
where waters countermingle.

The rushing past of feeling
no water surface mirrors.
A calm with unseen tremors
steels early ripples stealing.

Single love is never
and the waters cool and still.
Each every single on the mill
treads water, cold with fever.

On Seeing Ennerdale

All here is still and small beneath the morning:
below, the growing plaint of sky-born lambs.
The colours now of fox and vetch,
detergent shades of sheep and cattle
caught in sun above the many greens of fell.

We know stone walls enclose the mind,
but uncemented rocks
which stray like sheep
and merely prison time by being there?
Here time is called by keening birds
alone, on wings
pinned wide against the sky.

It's nice this view
calm, harsh, restful, not new.
We stop awhile
but not too long.
Against our backs the hard
motor of our discontent.

Some of us may understand nature's ways
name its parts, be knowledgeable
about the round of years.
Others camp on it, crampon-scratch its surface,
paint it, walk it.

But they don't stay,
and nor do we.
We turn our backs
on what we've left behind
to say that, yes,
we've been to Ennerdale.

South Bank

This city now does like a garment wear
the beauty of the morning, silent, bright.
From here the view uplifts, transports: light
autumnal softens, mutes, crosses water where
temples tower new, old, yet not amiss.
To reach this point one has to stalk
in half-light deep down beneath a bridge, walk
planks of mattress, take in the smell of piss.
Tested thus, reprieved perhaps, one looks towards
the other side transfigured, steeped, warmed in sun.
The city is both bricks and mortal, affords
its people space in which work and play are done.
Platforms, theatre, all human speech in words,
images of truth on stage, or by spin-doctors spun.

Palm Dove

Lost stranger from
    a distant land
alone its call
      unaccustomed
cadence impinging
    on the ear
each day at
    dawn and dusk
a signal sent
    but not received.

On looking down
    what will it see
a summer landscape
    not like its own
suffused with sounds
    but not its own:

its bubbling lament
    rising just before it falls.

Time & Space

Bells
ring no more
from the master's room,
or from other rooms
around the house.

Names
on the board,
'own bath', 'study', 'gun',
all sound like sounds
of sounds of sounds.

Passages
lead off dark,
faint
with the tread
of dusty feet.

Eyes
of stags
in an upstairs room
from blank walls
look straight ahead.

Taps
on baths
made for giant hands
now drip,
      and drip,
           and drip away.

War Memorial

We are so good at death.

Early morning suits this place.
Still white curving lines of stone
caught cold in sun.
The sleepers tucked beneath

soft green turf each
blade cut down to size.
Long ranks of men, comrades, friends
at rest, their duty done.

The words, fine words, engraved
in stone, marble, rise
above this quiet place
and speak a language known.

These quiet men have died.
The stones, the walls, the words
are there for good, lay bare
man's lasting cruelty to man.

We are so good at death.

School Photograph

There forever they will stand
or sit; stare glum, smile
fixed; some lost in thought, still
looking out as to some far distant

land. These young faces old
before their time. Yellow now
in black and white, they . . . how
sharply they come back. A story told

a second time. I know, and know
them not. For what they are is what
they were. Clear phantoms. Not
like at all what later comes, so

full of edges, shades and blur.
But where was I in all this
crowd? I must have had a place.
There . . . right at the end I sit, where

bent in studied crouch I know again
just what I thought. I posed,
scowled, wished and sought
to seem grown up. Down time's long

lane I make my way, but these flat
figures from the past will stay
young. For ever. Bright image matt.
It will always be their day.

Envy

A feeling provoked
by the arctic fox.
Unlike humans,
to survive in the wild
it has almost no needs.
Somehow intact
and without fear,
its life runs as
surroundings dictate.
For example its den,
dug into esker or pingo,
will last for up to
hundreds of years.
And, while humans struggle
with clothes and cold,
the arctic fox just
sheds, and grows
another coat.

Seemingly standing any cold
it lives its life
mysterious, almost ghostly,
flitting, whiter
even than the snow
across vast wastes:
unlike man, just posting
tiny clawmark signs,
to leave behind a landscape
in its unchanging
timeless pristine state.

Machair

A remaining, lasting
link with now
and what lies in the past.
For once, in human hands,
a landscape not exploited,
ruined.
Instead, by natural means
not only kept alive
and green, but
fertile, friendly
to the natural world.

Birds nest here
upon the ground,
remaining from machine-borne
death secure.
Flowers, plants, even
human crops live
side by side:
a rare example
of man's acceptance
of a harmony with
a landscape lived in,
but here at least
not just destroyed.

Frankfurt

I ask
where I am
on this rattly old tram.
'Bitte rücken Sie nach vorne durch.'
My case on the floor,
people look.

Where am I?
Why have I come?

Hauptwache . . . Dornbusch . . .
Ah! Weißer Stein!
Out, now! Down the steps.

It's really cold
and I'm back at school:
a 'Gymnasium'
is what they said
in that Ministry note.

So here I now am
shivering, green, and twenty-four.

Time

Should one go back
to where it all began?
I do not know,
I had not meant to.

But there it was,
that gate
the same old door.
Inside, no doubt,
the stairs
which took one up
to that first room,
an attic space
furnished, alien,
a place to stay,
but not remain.

They are there still,
the mortar and the bricks.

The past is done
yet suddenly re-evoked
by confrontation
with a surface world.

Love

Love
is
mysterious,
frightening.
It
comes
as
it
goes.
And
when
it's
gone,
it's
gone.
So that
what
is
left,
is
left.

Early Morning

I did so hate
to wake you up
lying there,
for once at peace,
innocent,
so like a child.

Yet your arms
went out
to press me on.

And though going away
was my intent
I now do wish I'd stayed.

Absent Presence

Today I breakfasted with you alone,
although you were not there.
I also spoke to you,
although you were not there.

And even if not one single
word was said,
I somehow felt you there.

I then sat on
at peace
quite still
listening,
registering
a sense,
and concord,
just all and ever new.

Filigree

A locket in a booklike shape,
intricate, metal, time-shadowed.
The covers, two locked doors
which never open, but enclose.
If worn, the locket
resting just above the heart
its purchase once provoked
holds a memory
firm
of love in trust.

Temporal

A wilting rose
placed on my desk
volcano-darkened red,
the petals curling at the edge
susceptible, sensitive to touch:
the texture
fragile, velvet, soft; all
seeming, gleaming, glowing;
an unspoken eternal mortal
and yet summer sense.

Mayday

The drive back,
downhill all the way.
Early morning sun
casting misty warmth
across the greening cold.
A blackbird rigid on
a naked branch-top,
beak frozen yellow mute.
In all this late-spring burst
a coloured alien flush,
a front, affront, contradiction
in the scene, between a surface
and the invisible unseen.

Casualty

A small toy car lying on its side,
all by itself
and in the grass.
Where is its owner?
Was it girl,
or boy?
I wandered on,
that image still in mind:
a small toy car left on its side.

Musings

A poem
is not just
think and thought

much less what
like would think.

A poem is
what feeling
thinks was thought.

A reality uncertain
intangible
but sought.

Models

Sitting at the doctor's
leafing through the gloss,
my eye was caught
by creatures, perhaps,
who knows, from outer space.

I tried just to imagine
what it was such poses
called to mind.
Nothing very normal or,
maybe, just clothes-horses
in some manic bind.

And now, much later,
what does the mind still see?
Contorted, dangling limbs,
faces extra, strange;
clothes hanging there
and from, as if somehow
unwittingly to imply
that fashion is both arbitrary
and,
as passing as the day.

Regarding a Church

Inside
more like
a building site.

Shivering
with damp and cold
one looks.

Drapes
over every window
close in.

Ahead
the altar, wooden
dusty, sharp.

Figures:
angels, disciples, simple
folk, their gaze

fixed
holy, upward, both
alien, familiar.

These
looks recognisable
from their

like
at churches one
has been to.

Moments
of unconscious conscious
deep unease.

The
secret, public viewer
is caught

between
the holy and the
artistic aim,

so
creeps away uncomforted,
uncomfortable

at
registering expectations
somehow unfulfilled.

The Silence of Snow

Feet sink soft
in the silent snow.
No sound.
No move.
Three crows
motionless
black
against the snow.
Sunflower heads
dead
hang
black
above the snow.
Distant firs curl down
bowing
silenced
by the snow surround.
No birds sing
and all the world
is still,
in silence bound.

Isolation

A lone pigeon
on a leafless branch
its feathers puffed

as snowflakes fall.
Motionless, unruffled,
almost fading

in the snow-filled
light, it remains
unmoving

seemingly unmoved
by what is
falling, falling,

from above.

Snowbunting

More like bird than flower,
a name to play with.
And just one of many
for that elfin bloom
of autumn, winter and of spring.
Like today, out in the lawn,
a tiny fragile nest of
crocus, slender, blue,
blue, almost transparent blue.

They peep just over and above
the wintry white of snow.
One, broken at the bud,
hangs, fragile, passing
as the light of day
yet, somehow, shy herald
of the spring to come.

The Language of Flowers

In a very old book
I found them:
flowers and words attached,
words linked in colour
and association:

Abatina – fickleness
Amaryllis – pride
Bluebell – constancy
Catchfly – snare.
They roused, these words
they provoked, they moved:

Wolfsbane – misanthropy
Aloe – grief
Hemlock – death
Harebell – submission.

Even flowers with names
to cherish:
Lobelia – malevolence
may bring harsh surprise
to a magical sound.

Or messages musical:
Dainty Rose – the smile I aspire to
Carnation Red – alas for my poor heart.
And later:
Weeping Willow – mourning.

Associations gather
so that at the end
with
Rosemary – remembrance
it all comes together;
echoes of flowers
which will ring
on and on, and which will
never cease to delight.

Irish Journey

The road flows red to the emptied sky
while goats stare down from slippery rock:
trees bending hug wind-bare slopes
in the falling gleam of rain-filled grass.

Loneliness makes its eloquent plea
to each touched fibre of remembered pain.

The still road glitters
as wheels spin west
where the sun dies again
in the clear mountain sky.

Definitions

It was not the word,
I think.
Or not that word.
Just, perhaps,
who knows?
The clear coldness of a word,
a word which cleared the air.
Like sun on early morning
cloud.
But clear it was.

Poetry

Indefinable,
a never-ending quest.
Like music
in sound but
essentially other.

Music has no need
of words,
for words can
confuse, convey, even
be musical,
yet confuse.
How does one, ideally,
communicate
emotions: inordinate,
inexplicable, lasting
latent?

There is no way
but forward in hopes
of creating that bridge
between
what is thought, felt,
and what is, may be,
somehow
in words passed on.

Yearning

A word to move the mind
a sense of searching
in the soul
visible
the soft fall of snow
the last glow the
slow passing of the sun
audible
the chorus of the early dawn
with ringing sounds
from single birds
which
echo
through the mind
to stir the heart
invisible intangible
yet
suddenly
within the realm
of seeming touch

Views

The camera never lies
is what we're always told.
Why then are we often
so surprised, or distressed?

One moment!
We and what?
Is it photographs
of others,
or those of ourselves?

But even with others,
for example, those famous,
does one not sometimes read
of retakes, countless, endless?

And in the matter of self
is what we see
the truth?
Or not just what we wish?

There perhaps may be the crux.
Pictures, portraits will
offer variety, depth.

A photograph has foreground,
perhaps something behind,
remains nonetheless surface
which time will uncover, date.
Later scrutiny inevitably
reveals a dated state.

So that however truthful,
photographs remain firmly fixed
in that one and only moment of time.

Effervescence

A play lasts
its just short span
though audiences
may take it home.

There
like a fire
it will burn
before
to ash it turns.

Unlike a fire
a play can
from its ashes rise,
re-ignite
in new-found form
to kindle and re-kindle
audiences anew.

And thus
rising from its past
a play may
spark
from fiery heart
new flames
to burn once more
and ever and again.

'Great Expectations'

What is it about a novel,
a great novel,
that never lets one go?
It captures, captivates,
engrosses, holds one
for ever in its thrall.

Perhaps, who knows,
is it at least
two aspects?
Familiarity and freshness?
One knows the plot, yet
is always caught once more,
may even identify
but each time
with an added extra.

Of course in identifying,
things change
as life moves on.

With Pip each reader
will react as instinct,
background, history do urge.

Such works cannot lose their
timeless never-ending pull,
provoke, inspire, enrich
the lives of all and one.
Inevitably reading continues,
so that never will there be
the shadow of a parting
of the ways.

Evanescence

I am at my table
looking out at rain,
the dimming glass of windows
helps ease away the strain.

Separation from outside
the world that passes by,
proceeds in utter silence
yet does not seem awry.

Cut off, glassed in, alone,
yet seeing through the glass
that others move along,
that they alone still pass,
I withdraw just ever more
behind that dimming glass.

Correspondence

In trying to bring some order
to suspended life,
I struggled through the motions
to face the task ahead.

Accumulations of life together
now forced a search and sift.
In one drawer all at once
a full package I did find.

Inside
were all the letters
sent down the years from me.

There totally and scrupulously
in keeping
they lay.

I hesitantly stretched
out a hand,
just slightly of one letter
the outer flap did raise.

I stopped.
The envelope I closed,
returned all
to where it had been kept.

I remained standing
as years from me were stripped.
A double sense of yearning,
as almost unthinking, I had dipped
into something which from my
possession
now had for ever passed.

Reflection

That picture of you alone
looking as only you can,
not straight
but straight towards
what only you do see.

That look which you alone
did have:
soft, warm, kind,
is still with me,
as indeed you are still.

Even that first fateful time
you looked
straight, direct,
and it was done,
stayed, which
and now alone, now
helps me forward, on my way.

'Sea Pictures'

Sounds, more sounds
and echoes,
footsteps on hard ground,
as memories arise,
each lasting, sharp, and round.

The voice, so near
rings out,
each every note, a tear,
as memories arise
to make that vision clear.

That music is no passing sound
and will onward roll,
like waves upon the sea
as memories arise,
and waves the shores do pound.

A Place in Time

It was what
she had wanted:
a quiet space
in the quiet earth.

And here I again now was,
registering
what I now beheld:
a quiet space
in the quiet earth,
and underneath a tree.

A simple wish,
now fulfilled.

Yet sight of that
space, covered,
all by itself,
disturbs.

Even more
to see the turf
above the urn
all brown and there, beside,
grey withered blooms.

Those two remains
above the ground
drove home a sense
of what it is to die:
one moment there,
the next no more.

Soon green will
mantle over what
remains beneath.

What's left is
now the past:
and remembrance

indelible

of someone loved
who cannot,
will not,
ever go away.

Brimstone

A sound which burns
like blood,
provokes pictures in the mind
of cauldrons boiling,
burning bright,
of tigers sulphurous,
forest furnaces of the night.

But before me in the air
a zephyred flicker,
yellow, tight, flitting
or rising-dipping on
bright velvet wings,
soft shimmer, fleeting, light.

A brimstone, in full flight,
above like-coloured forsythia
where from time to time
it briefly stops to alight.

Then once more like a flash
it continues on its wayward
way, until finally around
the corner of the house, is gone,
for wherever it is bound.

Differentials

Darkness and light
have us in their thrall,
whether fancy or fact
they are there for us all.

Not just with daylight
or what eyes do see
but what the mind catches,
in brightness perceives.

Darkness can lighten
if clear thoughts occur,
so the deep black of night
fades, to no longer deter.

An oncoming storm
with both darkness and light
exudes energy boundless,
can prodigiously form.

These two shades contrasting,
extremes extreme
complement, charismise
remain and, for all time,
become
even more than they seem.

Untimely Stirrings

All is still
and wintry black,
no snow or ice
upon the sill.

Birds even soft
begin to sing,
perhaps unwitting urge
to impel the spring.

And in the ground
dark, dank, all tight,
here and there, tiny
yellow flash of winter aconite.

Even catkins shining
bright, contrast with
winter darkling, may even
portend a coming of the light.

Cumulus

What does one see
when looking up at clouds?
Clear, startling in sunlight
so welcoming, soft.

If viewed from a plane,
clouds become seemingly
tangible, heaving, revolving,
almost beckoning ghosts.

But clouds can be dark,
threaten, foreboding,
to announce a billowing
tempest advance.

At nightfall often
winds do not blow.
Clouds then float still,
pale, pass away with the sun.

One goes with them home,
is surrounded in bed,
pillowed, fellowed, followed,
as they rest in one's head.

Surroundings

A sense of space
unconscious, conscious,
is always there
and all around.

How much depends
on what is in the mind.
Is one in the space,
or just of it?

Emotion also plays a role.
It can widen
if the mood provokes,
or contract
as spirits sink.

Mostly one is just
part,
instinctively
reacting and adjusting
to what is
there
and all around.

Places in Time

Whenever something happens
whatever that may be,
that place is there for ever
and for the mind to see.

Disappointments, tragedies
can never disappear.
They are held in place,
in one instant reappear.

Sometimes strange events
are there for one to see.
Once even an exam result
handed halfway up a tree.

Or that first time,
relief behind the rapture,
the years and what before,
on hold in lasting capture.

All poignancies are there
cannot, will not go away,
etched in the mind,
for one's ever lasting care.

Shadows

To read what one has written
can take one back in time,
one sees one as one was
because of that because.

Not that words have really changed.
One's senses may have sharpened,
One knows the one behind the words,
perhaps hears echoes of their chords.

Whatever ever may be said
is what words, all words, permit,
an approximation of what's there,
fallibility human, limit.

In spite, in deed, in every word,
the attempt to reach the heart
of emotion felt, impression clear,
from the whole down to each part.

The struggle goes on for ever
as words are sought and sought,
and feelings work to be expressed,
a struggle fought and fraught.

Artificial Flowers

seem sometimes
more genuine
than genuine.
For example, orchids.
Whiter than white
they may even have
a kind of scent,
and can last for ever:
inhuman
unfeeling
cold.

Almost like actors
who appear
larger than life
but who
in themselves
are sometimes
mere shells:
an exterior
for roles
slipped into
and out.

How strange
that perfection
remains
an aim:
understandable
human
but in itself
an artifice,
dead.

Grand Slam

As a spectator
one takes sides.
One plays oneself
in others
but rarely wonders.

One has perhaps
a favourite player.
Does one genuinely know why?
And does it really matter
who
in the end will win?

Out there those famous
are unrelated,
mean nothing personal.

Yet personal
they can become
in that being so superior
they convey
to others
what normal humans are:

uncontrolled
perfectly imperfect
just run of every mill.
In rare moments
of uncertainty
the best will
rise and rise,
so that even in adversity
they may waver briefly
even lose serenely,
but still come back to best.

The spectator may
even register
this,
hence be left
with widened mind
to recognize that
skill outstanding can
go way beyond the human,
to beckon and inspire.

Communication

A letter comes.
How nice, one thinks,
in hopes of hope.

Instead of which
just words and words,
the phrases spread

like jam on bread
soft, moist, eminently
digestible:

"Hope to see"...
"Are you well?"...
"Yes, is it not?"...

The phrases flow,
not good, not bad,
then just go on,
and on,
until
even they do not.

Self-Discipline

One lies in bed
and works it out.
Today, yes, today
it's got to start.

It's so pleasant
just lying there,
thinking it out,
with time to spare.

And all about what
one is going to do.
Hard, stiff routine
yes, ready to go.

Then one gets up,
the day has begun.
Now we will start,
it has to be done.

But first a good
breakfast, and after,
we'll see. Too much,
too fast, goes against the grain.

These things need planning,
nothing to gain from overdone rush.
Who knows, it could go wrong
if there's too hard a push.

And the very next day,
lying in bed, so good to plan
for things healthier, better,
but … in time,
if one genuinely, still can.

Means Test

What is it with money
that never goes away?
Unless you never worry,
and then have none to pay.

But those without,
we're told, live well
above their means, at least
that maybe limited spell.

Until they crash,
but then emerge
if not with credit, yet
still they've had their bash.

While others worry,
scrimp and save
for that day rainy
on the stony path they pave.

How does one better live?
Foregoing, frugal, surly
or lackadaisically foolish and,
to hell with all the hurley.

The Brooch

A simple seal
not forged.

Bands not signed
delivered.

Crossed brass sounds
which echo.

Obituary

"John Lindley has died"
is all
that tiny notice said.
Four words to end a life:
full stop.

One whole life
in just four words.
How bleak,
almost, indeed blank:

a whole life
written off
in just four words.

Inside Belsen

A body resting
uneasily against the rails
head bent sideways
mouth
half-open rigid
a seeming smile
frozen there
in black and white.

One looks, aware
of regarding someone
dead
unknown
forsaken
gone.

A picture
time
a fate
imposed on so many
innocent
drawn in
and then
for all time
lost.

Eating Alone

One takes out items just
for one, plate, cup, knife, spoon,
needs are no must
for one, just one single one.

Where shall one eat,
in the kitchen, on one's feet?
Or at table, just to stare
anywhere, but just there.

One sits where one sits,
there just, not a look
towards one seat empty, left,
one eats, one must, even if bereft.

And when one has done
one gets to one's feet,
goes out with the crumbs,
possibly, just possibly, replete.

Lives

It is worst for those whose mouths are closed,
who speak but in the safety of their minds
and, smiling, walk the world
with faces, masks on moods they do not show.

What mean – kind, warm hearted –
when in those few moments
in which lives are made
come stammered words to say
what others want to hear?

They do not wish to hurt
nor, though different,
step across the minds of most.

Thus sparing others
they break inside, and
damn themselves to lives of lies,
not always big,
evasions nonetheless.

One wonders
at the last
on looking back
will they still see
the way they've come?

Or will the clinkered habits
of the years
reduce even awareness
of the final state
to instinct, unfelt tugs
at all sense of what once was?

For Rolf

Why must the kindest go?

Are we better, more wise,
or just more cold,
insensitive to much that lies outside?

He was different
even in the way he looked.

His white clown face, sharp,
pale the high-ridged cheek
putting us beyond its pale.

And underneath
a spirit of such warmth, though
with itself no quarter chink.

We wavered,
stopped at a fence,
or passed it on the easy side.

While he
kept looking
inward,
at some motive light
which burned itself,
but not to die.

His standards were not mine.
I know because I stood back,
was with him least.
One heard of him, so little saw.

There were of course the others
who, caring,
stood by him to the last.

They buried him.

It rained that day,
or so I heard,
a drab, wet, taking leave.
The weather,
a commonplace
on a common place of death.

Why must the kindest go?

Shades of Grey

A somehow phrase,
contradictory perhaps,
since grey really
is a shade,
and shades.

Yet there are so
many shades of shade,
and shading grey.
One might think of
human hair which
greys from light to dark.

Or clouds which
yet may offer shade,
stride across the sky,
to swell and die.

Or in the mind,
as thoughts appear,
sometimes light,
but which then soon
can turn to grey.

This is a phrase
which pales
its way,
and works through
all the many shades of grey.

Autumn

It has all
been said before.
But still it comes,
each year it comes.

To bring a sense,
awareness,
that another year
will soon be gone.

The beauty, colour,
deep reds and brown,
before deepening pallor
as, down and down.

A passing mood, suspended time,
before the snow, with freezing rime.

Late Beauty

Just looking at this flower,
the name it matters not,
mere reverential sense
of nature's essence, power.

The single round bloom soft
each petal perfect, slim,
colour gentle, pale.
One looks again, and oft.

Yet this year small, and
smaller, the autumn of its stay.
There will be no more spring
in the winter of its day.

Happenstance

Turning on the heating
I thought suddenly
of a bumble-bee I'd seen

hanging, crooked, curled
up against, inside
an autumn flower.

Outside in that field.
It was still alive,
just, but soon to die:

the cold autumn damp
working into and against.
And as I then walked

through warming space
I reflected once more
on that tiny mass

curled up against,
inside an autumn bloom,
also soon to fade away.

Simplicity

Some ring-doves on the ground,
disturbed, whirl,
wings whistling, off.

Not far,
they land in trees,
sway with the leaves,
look round.

As if to imply
we have it all
just here.

They do not know,
as every move
is just as nature says.

They fly, settle,
sleep, and merely
wait for what
will come by day,
or night.

Mating

On the white wall
like filaments
black, exquisitely
slender, almost
geometrically set.

Not only long
thin, end to end,
but held, transfixed
together.

No move, no sign
or agitated stir
at all.

Yet new life
is on the brink
brought about by
just two crane flies
dark against the white
of wall.

www.

I saw, rippling
in the air,
a tiny thread,
so thin and spare.

Part of a web, elastic
tight, glistening
colours, rainbow,
subtle in the light.

That seeming soft
and tender thread,
which nonetheless traps,
wraps round the dead.

Horizons

Gazing up, as one does
up, up, and into sky
blue, bright, intense
towering, endless.

That unfathomable infinite,
an element vanishing, vague,
up into which one yearns, aspires:
tiny, earthed, a mere speck and dot.

Yet an indescribable sense,
sensation tense, takes its grip:
"… incomparable purity of the azure,
with no steelier point than infinity."

All About

Just beyond
is where it is:
not visible
not audible
but that's where it is.

You register,
even perhaps sense,
constantly strive
to reach out,
reach it.

It does not show.
How, why should it?
To see, hear and know,
would that then
be it?

Or, far worse, clear
view, or sight:
no call then
for straining more
towards the light.

Night Thoughts

All is black
no sound, no move.
One lies, held by,
inside, that thrall.

One wants to
slip away, to sleep.
But thoughts swift
random, unclear
clear, impose
and steer.

One lies so
still, silenced,
emotion stirred,
direction dim.

Inside one shrinks
as visions part:
"... like the painting of a sorrow,
a face without a heart."

Standing Alone

is what we all
do,
even if and when
we
are not alone.

Yet sometimes
one
can together be
even more alone
than
if one is
just alone.

How does one
then
live?

In oneself?
Outside oneself?

There is an
answer,
but for each
it must, can
only be found
alone.

Second-hand

It was in the window
of a shop,
not far from where I work.

A book by me.
I bought it,
not because of need,
just curious, and struck.

I looked inside
and saw the name:
a colleague, friend.
The dedication said it all.

I walked away
in deepest thought
and wondered, wondered
as I went.

I did not even like
to hold that book,
familiar yet unfriendly.

It had been simply
sold for cash.
A colleague and a friend.

Down in the Cellar

In search of something
else, I saw it:
a household item
I would need.

Then it struck
and struck again,
how I'd been cared
for, down the years.

Even if now time
had passed,
it all came
rushing back:

that sense of
being loved,
and cared for,
even after long
parting of the ways.

Suspense

A slow room,
no movement,
even the silence
is still.

All the books in
rows stir not,
they just all
stand still.

The curtains, chairs,
a table,
motionless
are still.

Leaves of plants
on a window-sill
stand each alone,
remaining still.

And I not moving,
take this in,
just breathe
stay still, quite still.

Valediction

No leaves on graves
but all around.
No movement
except one robin
among leaves falling,
far behind the graves.

Beyond the graves,
outside the grove,
dull traffic waves
murmur further, further
and way above.

The graves are still,
and all around
leaves fall, fall,
but make no sound.

One comes, strays,
to leave and wonder.

A Picture

Just one fleeting glance will do.
Two flowers in a vase.
Nothing could be simpler,
and yet they draw one in.

The flowers are still,
white, motionless, right.
The vase tall, also softly
white. It rises, rises

all around those flowers white.
The frame is also coloured
thus, all embracing, even
if no heart is seen.

There one stands, transfixed,
by two white flowers in a vase
all still, suddenly soft
centre of an impassioned world.

Parting

The past, a strange land
so far away, yet here.
Every day will take away
what once there was.

It comes, and thrusts,
as eyes, mind, wander:
alights, reflects, but
then sinks back.

Moments, feelings, even
close touch to touch:
here once again, but
then no more.

So now each day much
and even more alike,
will thrust one back to
hold again what once one
likes to think was there.

Into the Night

On leaving the house
at that moment of sound.
Down below, even the ground
shakes at the boom of the bell.

Out in the dark, those deep
quivering peals penetrate
down into soul, as if
poised all to reveal.

One stands there rock still,
tolls pounding into the ground
as if darkness was light, and
revelation on quiver all around.

A Moment

Two clouds
moving across
an empty sky –
blue, blue,
unending blue.

And down below,
down, down deep
a sense of
essence, of something
there,
intangible, floating –

almost like two clouds
moving across
an empty sky.

Lives

How does one make out
the way that
one has come?
So much depends on
chance,
on turning
left,
or turning right.

Only later, much,
may things start
to clear,
as what was
somehow emerges,
a seeming pattern,
even if
there was none.

All Things Bright

Spring each year,
when colours clear,
both young and sheer
do strike, strike,
and strike again.

They resonate, and echo
years long past,
remind of what
once was,
will be again,
when all else gone.

A beauty, fresh,
eternal,
passing,
but unlike life,
each year
rising from the dead,
re-born.

Silent Night

Is it just the lack of sound?
Or standing there and all alone?
Or even in a crowd full bound,
held still, and on their own.

Or out with nature in the night
where things surround, envelop all.
No birds sing, encroachment tight,
not one tree quivers, however tall.

Or in a dream locked in fight,
held fast, hands tied?
Mouth tightly shut, no light,
a never-ending soundless tide.

Perhaps lips even strain to scream
but no sound comes to end this dream.

Leaves

April is a cruel month.
It warms, it cools,
it kills.

Out in the garden
where all was green
now is partly brown
or deadly black.

Overnight it struck.

One moment
all was well but,
as in life,
all can change,
from deepest green
to darkest night.

Art

A three letter word,
so easily spelt.

And there it all is
out there, in there,
unmade beds, wedded
bricks, pots and bedpans.

Unavoidable,
overlookable. Emin-
ently penetrable,
from firstlings
to Hirstlings.

Art today:
a never ending
three letter word.

Not by Name

For that was not his way.

His is a living presence
and all who knew
can see him still.

That look which
went
from him to those
whom reaching was his warmest hope.

To friends – one thinks
to all –
he was himself.
Example, friend, and more.

He lived each book,
would hint, reveal, unveil
not point.

The listeners listened,
minds widening
like ripples on a pool.

He let them go,
waters which ripple still.

Perceptions

Looking in a mirror,
what is reflected there?
Or rather, is what stares at us
what we prefer to see?

Age may play a role,
one changes on one's way.
In early life, the wish to be,
perhaps even through appearance, seem.

Then later, thoughts move on
towards re-creation, signs
of what once may have been,
wished wishes back to what once was.

The light goes off,
the image fades, to leave
behind some slight apprehension
of what once one thought was there.

Reflection

Looking at that picture
of a child.
It looks, and looks.
If looks could tell.
But those looks can't,
because a child will
see, but hardly know.
The eyes wide open,
empty. Just.
Yet full.

As what is seen
is there, but not
to grasp.

And in that face,
unmoving, moved,
an innocence in thrall.

Blackcap

There are so many birds
in spring, so many sing.
One sits outside, leans back,
as sounds just ring and ring.

All at once another voice
rippling, rising then
so full, so supple clarion-clear.
But where can that bird just be?

It was invisible, even if behind
leaves something moved.
Until one day it revealed itself
before again it was no more.

Not true. Invisible but audible,
the notes all ringing clear –
as if only behind a leafy screen
could such a song be made to hear.

A Nest in Time

Those tiny birds come,
those tiny birds go,
how their wings drum
as they fast to and fro.

Not a sound to be heard
as through the pane
one sees each tiny bird
search for food it must gain.

Behind the glass
where all is warm,
one watches birds pass
in face of constant elemental harm.

Appearances

Two avenues of beeches
in early summer green
foliage glittering
create a seeming natural sheen.

Behind the lines of trees
above and in the sky,
impeccable range of blue,
no clouds impede the view.

Yet way up there above
where swallows, swifts would fly,
one looks, and looks in vain,
to see nothing but empty sky.

Equally bare the fields so green
where flowers used to bloom,
a realisation that what is there
merely covers an empty scene.

Jo Rippier was born in Plymouth. After attending
King's School, Worcester, he went up to Cambridge.
For most of his career he was a lecturer in the
English Department of Goethe-Universität
Frankfurt, where he was also much involved in
theatre, and where a number of his plays were
performed.